SURVIVING *grief*

SANDY ZAUGG

Pacific Press® Publishing Association
Nampa, Idaho
Oshawa, Ontario, Canada
www.pacificpress.com

Cover and inside design by Aaron Troia
Cover art from iStockphoto.com

Copyright © 2010 by Pacific Press® Publishing Association
Printed in the United States of America
All Rights Reserved

You can obtain additional copies of this book by calling toll-free 1-800-765-6955
or by visiting http://www.adventistbookcenter.com.

Scriptures quoted from TLB are from *The Living Bible,* copyright © 1971 by Tyndale House
Publishers, Wheaton, IL. Used by permission.

Library of Congress Cataloging-in-Publication Data:

Zaugg, Sandra L., 1938-
  Surviving grief : a personal journey / Sandy Zaugg.
      p. cm.
  ISBN 13: 978-0-8163-2400-2 (pbk.)
  ISBN 10: 0-8163-2400-X (pbk.)
  1. Grief. 2. Loss (Psychology) 3. Bereavement—Psychological aspects. I. Title.
  BF575.G7Z38 2010
  155.9'37—dc22

2010025621

10 11 12 13 14 • 5 4 3 2 1

DEDICATION

This book is dedicated to all the wonderful friends
who helped my children and me through our times of sorrow.
Some of you are mentioned in this book,
but all of you are remembered in my heart.

OTHER BOOKS BY SANDY ZAUGG

CONTENTS

When Tragedy Strikes

Looking back through my tears, I realize I was fortunate. My husband and I had a chance to say all the things we wanted to say. To be exact, we had eleven months after the diagnosis until the cancer ran its course. Wayne guided me in what I needed to do after his death. For instance, we had an old Volvo station wagon that worked well—only because he knew how to keep it repaired. Although Wayne had been a college professor for fourteen years, he was,

One FACES AN OVER-WHELMING SHOCK AND DISBELIEF WHEN A LOVED ONE DIES SUDDENLY.

first and always, a farm boy from Iowa who knew how to fix things. He wanted my first purchase after his funeral to be a new car, a reliable car. He even specified the make and model.

Wayne talked with our children and said Goodbye to friends. He even asked a colleague to take him to the college campus just four weeks before he died so that he could talk to his chemistry students about being prepared to die—at any age.

Not everyone is so lucky. For some, a phone call from a hospital or a police officer at the door may be the first indication that anything is wrong. One faces an overwhelming shock and disbelief when a loved one dies suddenly—whether through a heart attack, a random act of violence, or an auto accident. And I remember . . . I remember kneeling in the gravel at the side of a busy road, nine years after my husband's death, holding the not-quite-dead body of my twenty-two-year-old son. I will never forget the shock . . . the horrified disbelief . . . and the soul-wrenching grief when he died three days later.

You PROMISED ME STRENGTH AND COURAGE, I OFTEN REMINDED GOD. JUST HELP ME GET THROUGH THE NEXT FEW MINUTES, THE NEXT HOUR.

You promised me strength and courage, I often reminded God. *Just help me get through the next few minutes, the next hour.*

By my sharing my climb out of devastating grief, I hope you will be helped in your own struggle. And I hope that sharing my really stupid mistakes will help you avoid similar pitfalls.

GRIEVING, COPING, AND SURVIVING

Many books tell about grief in great detail, but this book is written to help with your recovery. However, it's helpful to review what comes first. No one's story of grief is exactly like another person's, but there are five commonly accepted steps in the grieving process for adults:

1. Denial and isolation. *This is just a bad dream. If I ignore it, it will go away. I'm so alone. People must be able to tell by just looking at me that I'm different from what I was yesterday.*

2. Anger. At God, at your spouse's job, at your mother-in-law, at the bus driver, and at your cat . . . anger at anything and everything.

3. Bargaining. With God, with the doctor, or with yourself. *If you keep him alive, Lord, I'll go to church every week for the rest of my life and give lots of money to the poor.*

4. Depression and withdrawal. The all-encompassing sadness. *Nobody* *understands; no one else has ever had it as hard as I do. Nothing will ever be right again.*

5. Acceptance. You can admit your loss out loud and stop setting the extra place at the table, although you still will occasionally fix too much food.

Not everyone progresses neatly through the list. Some experience these steps in a different order. And most of us will experience an initial numbness that helps us through the first few days, usually until right after the funeral.

Following the funeral, we may exist in a fog for a week or two. We may do silly things without even knowing it. For instance, I might go to the store for milk and return with cough syrup. Or step into the shower and forget to take off my clothes. Or tuck my kids' socks neatly into the freezer! During this time, kind friends (or my sister) would say things such as "What is it you're doing today?" or "How's your laundry?" or "What are you planning to cook for supper?" They helped me focus on the realities of my life and on responsibilities. They never asked me why I threw my favorite blouse into the trash or why I sat staring out the window while the bathtub overflowed.

My children grieved, too, but their grief took very different forms.

A few hours after my husband, Wayne, died, my eight-year-old daughter's emotions exploded. One moment she snuggled in my arms, sobbing; the next she raced through the house beating her small fists on anything that came within reach. She beat on the walls, her books, the dog, her brother, and her cousins.

After about ten minutes, her anger subsided for an hour or two, then began all over. During the funeral, instead of having her beside me, my sister and I arranged to have her sit between two very large young men whom she loved dearly. Then if she started acting out during the funeral, one of them could just wrap his strong arms around her and carry her out.

More than a week went by before her anger subsided. I often had to bite my tongue to keep from scolding her for such behavior. But the angry outbursts

Let's FACE FACTS: LIFE ISN'T FAIR.

were an important expression of her sadness and loss. She needed to act out before she could channel her grief into a more socially acceptable form.

My thirteen-year-old son, on the other hand, grieved quietly. For several weeks he and his dog sat on a hillside for hours each day, staring into the distance. He seldom spoke to anyone. Seldom cried.

I felt so helpless. I didn't know how to reach him. Sometimes I'd sit with him. But I couldn't seem to draw him out. In the end, I waited more than a month before he reached out and began sharing his feelings and taking an interest in life again.

Whether for child or adult, be aware that not all the steps in the grieving process apply to everyone. I evidently skipped the anger phase. I never yelled at God and asked, "Why me?" I came to the conclusion long before that if it's going to happen to anyone, why not me? Let's face facts: Life isn't fair.

Even Wayne's cancer was unfair. To have colon cancer, one is supposed to be over sixty, a heavy meat eater, and a couch potato. Well, Wayne died at forty-one, a lifelong vegetarian who climbed mountains for fun. No, life isn't fair.

Coping With Private Grief

It's important that we take time for our private grief. And our grief begins when we first get the bad news; it doesn't necessarily wait for the actual death. So, if you need to run through the house screaming (as one of my friends did), be sure your family is out of the house.

For me, grief was quieter. I often stood in the shower with the water running so my children wouldn't hear me cry. I was the cleanest woman in town.

According to my sister, the children and I sat together frequently during those first few months after Wayne's death, talking about their daddy and crying together. I have no recollection of doing that—but I'm glad we did it. It's necessary to allow children time to grieve.

If running through the house screaming or standing in the shower isn't your style, try journaling. It's considered one of the best aids in coping when your life is out of control. Buy an inexpensive, not-too-big spiral notebook and pour your heart into it. Write down your thoughts, your problems, and your hurts. Don't pay any attention to spelling, grammar, or even coherent sentences. Just let it flow. When you are ready to sell one of your children to the lowest bidder, write. When you are so lonely you'd marry the first homeless derelict you see, write. Somehow, getting emotions and frustrations down on paper seems to reduce their impact and make them more manageable. And according to counselors, it's good therapy.

It's IMPORTANT THAT WE TAKE TIME FOR OUR PRIVATE GRIEF.

Journaling, however, doesn't work for everybody. My friend Jeanette said journaling depressed her. It reinforced her sadness and despair. So she turned to reading—as I did. A good mystery and a bathtub filled with hot water (after the children were asleep) lifted my spirits and helped me to escape my reality for a while.

One person I know found that music was a good outlet. After her children were tucked in bed, she'd put her favorite music on the stereo and turn out the lights. The pathos of the symphony brought first tears, then a calmness to her soul.

In the past, I had prided myself on crying no more than once a year—whether I needed to or not, I'd tell friends. After my husband's cancer diagnosis, that all changed. To my embarrassment and frustration, no matter how hard I tried to suppress them, tears were always just barely below the surface, spilling over at the most inopportune times—when I was walking down the aisle in a supermarket, when a friend told a funny story, and when I served supper.

 *Try* JOURNALING.

Perhaps if I had allowed myself to cry more at the right times, I might have had drier eyes other times. We need to allow ourselves time to weep, to learn coping skills, and to cherish our memories before we can begin to think about the future.

BITTERSWEET REMEMBERING

"My son had the ugliest feet you can imagine!" I chuckled—even as a small sob escaped me, and I wiped my tears. "And he took photographs of them in Moscow and London and Singapore and Indonesia . . . and anywhere else he visited."

"I'm so sorry," my friend said. "I didn't mean to make you cry."

"Don't apologize; I'm the one who mentioned Ed," I replied. "You should have seen him! We walked out of the airport in Moscow, and he immediately unpacked his camera equipment. Then he slipped off his shoes and jumped up on a cement wall. He stretched out his long legs and shot a picture of the city skyline between his bare feet." My friend laughed with me.

My husband and son were a big part of my life—half my family, in fact. I couldn't—and shouldn't—just remove them from my speech and memories.

Not long after my husband died, I began occasionally tossing an appropriate anecdote about him into a conversation, as I would have done if he were alive. If you do the same, you need to know that it sometimes causes awkwardness. I found that after my husband died, most people never mentioned him in my presence. In fact, some reacted with shock when I did. Now my friends are used to it. And if they knew Wayne, they may throw in a special remembrance of their own.

I did the same thing after my son died and found college students eager to share their memories of Ed. I hope it helped them in their healing processes; I know it helped me.

Sensitive friends waited for cues from me that I was ready to talk and remember. When I initiated a memory of Wayne in a conversation, it freed them to remember

It TOOK A WHILE FOR ME TO REALIZE THAT MY HUSBAND'S FRIENDS AND COLLEAGUES WERE GRIEVING TOO.

him too. It also allowed me a chance to support them in their grief. Sharing stories and tissues was healing to all of us.

This surprised me at first. I thought only of my own grief and that of my children, not of our friends, who were also suffering. It took a while for me to realize that my husband's friends and colleagues were grieving too.

Think what it would be like if we couldn't talk about our loved one. We would have to avoid all subjects that might lead to remembrances. This means that I personally would have to avoid any discussion of mountain climbing, rock climbing, sailing, gardening, photography, camping, surfing, guitars, basketball, and ugly feet.

None of this is suggesting that every conversation should dwell on the past. Definitely not. But if something about your loved one comes up naturally in a conversation, don't shy away from it. If you have young children, these may be the only remembrances they'll have of their daddy, brother, or auntie.

Some folks will, of course, balk at hearing any reference to the loved ones they've lost. When I notice it, I try to be sensitive to their discomfort. Each person handles loss in his or her own way.

But IF SOMETHING ABOUT YOUR LOVED ONE COMES UP NATURALLY IN A CONVERSATION, DON'T SHY AWAY FROM IT.

When it hurts to remember, I sometimes allow myself to feel the stabbing pain and experience the tears and sorrow—for a little while. Then I have a talk with the Lord and ask Him to help me to channel my thoughts in a different direction—and I get busy. I might do dishes—there are always dishes in my sink. Or I call a friend about going out to lunch. Or I watch an Agatha Christie mystery on TV. Or I focus on a memory that makes me smile. Like the one where my patient husband took over the cooking duties on our camping trips—after I set a national Forest Service picnic table on fire. I was just trying to get our one-burner camp stove to work. I felt so stupid and inept, but some of my women

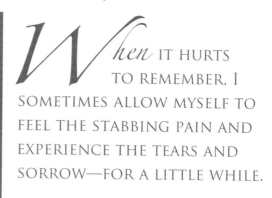

When IT HURTS TO REMEMBER, I SOMETIMES ALLOW MYSELF TO FEEL THE STABBING PAIN AND EXPERIENCE THE TEARS AND SORROW—FOR A LITTLE WHILE.

friends envied me when they saw Wayne cooking on the camp stove on our next outing. They said I'd been pretty smart to set the fire.

While my guilt over the fire went away quickly, other types of guilt do not go away so easily.

MISPLACED GUILT

My husband was in so much pain before his death that I begged God to let him just go to sleep. Then Wayne died, and I felt guilty about it—like it was somehow my own fault. I prayed the same prayer after my son's accident when he had a series of cardiac arrests and his brain flatlined. More guilt.

Unexpected problems arose when I tried to balance my memories with the new path my life was taking. When I emptied Wayne's clothes from the closet we'd shared, I felt like my heart would break in two—but I also felt guilty, though I didn't know why. Perhaps because I was moving on with my life, or perhaps because I was giving away something that had been part of him. (I did keep one of his jackets.) I experienced guilt the first time I laughed after his death—it somehow seemed wrong to be able to laugh when Wayne was dead.

I certainly felt guilty the first time I went out to dinner with a gentleman friend, even though eighteen months had elapsed since Wayne's death. By the way, when I returned home from that dinner, my fourteen-year-old son stood at the door with one hand on his hip. "Where have you been?" he asked sternly. (This was a bit of role reversal!) He knew where I'd gone and with whom I'd gone and it wasn't late—it was only nine o'clock! Of course, that made me feel guilty for neglecting my children.

I even felt guilt when I took the kids to Disneyland two years after Wayne's death. I think I have an overactive guilt complex!

My marriage was a contract. "Until death do us part," we had vowed. Now that Wayne was dead, I wasn't married. The contract was over. But my heart clung to my husband and my marriage. I sometimes even pretended he was still alive.

When I EMPTIED WAYNE'S CLOTHES FROM THE CLOSET WE'D SHARED, I FELT LIKE MY HEART WOULD BREAK IN TWO—BUT I ALSO FELT GUILTY, THOUGH I DIDN'T KNOW WHY.

Finally, I had to sit myself down and say, "Look, Wayne's gone. He's not here. Now it's time to rejoin the human race—guilt free!"

Surely God has more for us to do than look back and weep.

FOCUS ON THE FUTURE

The intense grief will lessen in a few months to a year or so, and the memories of those sad times will return with less frequency as time goes by, but they *will* continue to come and go. Years later I wept silently at my daughter's wedding, picturing her father beside her as she walked down the aisle. Even as I'm writing this, I'm wiping tears, remembering how much I missed his unflappable presence in the waiting room when our first grandchild was being born. Now, more than twenty years after my husband's death, I occasionally still remember and wipe a tear. The honest truth is that grief never entirely goes away.

When my memories hurt too much, I grab an atlas or my box of maps and plan a trip. The hard part is tailoring it to fit my budget and schedule—if I should actually take the trip. In any case, it gives me something to look forward to. I've yet to see the Statue of Liberty or Mount Rushmore or Death Valley or the Alamo. And though I've had the opportunity since

Wayne died to travel quite a bit in Asia and Europe, I still haven't seen Greece nor been on a safari in Africa nor floated on the Amazon River. The possibilities are endless—even if my bank account isn't.

Looking forward keeps me from spending all my time looking back and longing for the company of people I don't have anymore. When I look back for very long, I sink into self-pity and wallow in my sadness

The INTENSE GRIEF WILL LESSEN IN A FEW MONTHS TO A YEAR OR SO, AND THE MEMORIES OF THOSE SAD TIMES WILL RETURN WITH LESS FREQUENCY AS TIME GOES BY, BUT THEY *WILL* CONTINUE TO COME AND GO.

and become totally self-absorbed. That really isn't the way I want to live for the rest of my life. Focusing on the past seems like a one-way ticket to deep depression. After all, I have a wonderful, caring daughter and a delightful granddaughter who are still alive.

Then in God's all-wise timing, as I'm reaching for a tissue, the phone rings. I give a loud sniff, wipe my red, swollen eyes, and say a shaky "H-Hello?"

And a tiny voice says, "You coming for Christmas, Gramma? Huh? We have a present for you. You come, OK, Gramma?" And I realize the future is still there. Bright, enthusiastic, and almost four years old.

Cherish YOUR MEMORIES AND, AT THE SAME TIME, REACH OUT FOR NEW EXPERIENCES—MAKE NEW MEMORIES FOR THE FUTURE. BUT MOST OF ALL, CHERISH THE LOVED ONES YOU STILL HAVE WITH YOU.

Cherish your memories and, at the same time, reach out for new experiences—make new memories for the future. But most of all, cherish the loved ones you still have with you.

Doing the Hard Stuff

My hard stuff began before Wayne died. During the last six weeks of his life, Wayne needed Demerol shots for his pain every three hours, night and day. (That was the medication available back then. I understand there are much better, longer-acting medications these days.) Now, I'm not the least bit medically inclined and had never given, nor desired to give, an injection. So the day my nurse-friend Priscilla marched into my kitchen with an orange, a syringe filled with water, and a vial of Demerol remains indelibly etched on my mind.

My hard stuff began before Wayne died.

My memory of this scene may not be totally accurate. I know now that she must have had a number of syringes with her, perhaps an entire box. But I was too shocked to be a rational observer.

"Here," she said, holding out the orange and the water-filled syringe to me, "shoot this."

"No, I can't!" I wailed, backing away. "I know what you're thinking—and there's no way I can give Wayne shots!"

Calmly, she wrapped my fingers around the orange and spoke with authority. "The doctor says Wayne needs a shot every three hours—around the clock. You've got to learn to give them, or he'll have to go to the hospital tomorrow."

"But I can't! I can't!" Tears streamed down my face.

I could barely see the orange through my tears as she overrode my objections.

In quick succession, I gave practice injections to both the orange and Priscilla. Then a real one to Wayne. It was three days before I could give him the required shot without crying!

There was one thing Priscilla didn't warn me about. Giving injections to Wayne was so important and such intense times for me that it was three years after his death before I quit waking up at midnight, three, and six.

Often when tragedy faces us, we are called upon to perform feats we would never dream of doing in earlier, happier times of our lives. So what's the best thing to do? Take a deep breath and say, *OK, Lord, I can't do this without You. So help me, please.* Then just do it. We really have no other option.

A text in 1 Corinthians helped me through this period. Granted, I twisted the literal meaning a bit, but it was comforting to me. So here is 1 Corinthians 10:13, Sandy's version: "You can trust God, who will not permit you to receive more trials than you can stand. But when you are overwhelmed, He will also give you a way to escape so that you *will* be able to stand it."

Of course, there were more than a few times when I questioned God about His perception of my ability to cope. But He always sent support when I needed it most—like Priscilla, for instance. It took me a while to realize that God had more faith in me than I did.

I could have categorically refused to give an injection, though that's

> *Often* WHEN TRAGEDY FACES US, WE ARE CALLED UPON TO PERFORM FEATS WE WOULD NEVER DREAM OF DOING IN EARLIER, HAPPIER TIMES OF OUR LIVES.

difficult to do when you are faced with a determined nurse. Had I refused, Wayne would have been admitted to the hospital six weeks earlier than necessary, or a nurse-friend would have had to show up at our door every three hours, day and night. That would have burdened friendship to the breaking point.

I'm also glad Priscilla warned me that Demerol "talks." "Wayne may say things totally out of character. Unfair things," she said. "But remember, it's the Demerol talking, not Wayne. So don't even bother defending yourself."

It TOOK ME A WHILE TO REALIZE THAT GOD HAD MORE FAITH IN ME THAN I DID.

A few days later, when I fell exhausted on to the bed (after the midnight injection) beside my always-loving husband, it began. "You know this cancer is your fault," he said in the darkness. I was stunned! Then I remembered Priscilla's wise words and bit my tongue. But he continued, "If you hadn't insisted we have children, I wouldn't have been under so much stress, and this wouldn't have happened."

What is he talking about? He loves his children—and I didn't insist on having them. I wanted to shout at him and tell him he was crazy! That he was making it all up! Again, I remembered. No sense arguing with the Demerol. So I rolled over and pretended to sleep.

More Hard Stuff

Another very difficult task was telling the children about their dad's diagnosis. We decided that honesty was the best policy; then if he lived, they could rejoice in the miracle God performed. If he died, they would be somewhat prepared. Our son was twelve and our daughter seven when the cancer was first diagnosed, old enough to know what was going on. Besides, we were a family, for better or worse.

After WAYNE'S DEATH, I WAS SURPRISED TO FIND THAT ONE OF THE HARDEST THINGS FOR ME TO DO WAS TO GO TO BED.

Some friends criticized our decision to tell the children, saying we had placed an unnecessary burden on them. But kids are smart. They quickly figure out when something is very wrong. And they know when adults are keeping secrets. So their imaginations conjure up horrendous possibilities, though probably not worse than reality in this case.

You know your children best. What would be good for them?

In the wake of your loss, even relatively small problems loom large when you have to deal with them alone. After Wayne's death, I was surprised to find that one of the hardest things for me to do was to go to bed. No one had prepared me for this trauma. You may handle it differently than I did, but if you lose a spouse, you have to face it.

Lying alone in a queen-sized bed night after night was a constant reminder to me of the emptiness in my life. I'd hug pillows and cry for hours. Finally, I got rid of my big bed and bought a twin-sized bed. I put a new stack of books beside the bed and crawled in. That first night I read 'til dawn. Gradually, I fell asleep earlier and earlier, until I sometimes read only a half hour or so before dropping off to sleep. It has become such a habit that I suspect I will always read before I fall asleep.

IF YOU TRY READING, BE PARTICULAR ABOUT THE BOOKS YOU CHOOSE.

If you try reading, be particular about the books you choose. If you lost your spouse and the book is a romance, it needs to be a light one. A sensual, moving love story can send you right back to crying in your pillows. A horror story can keep you awake all night, hearing strange noises.

Of course, if you choose anything that is at all exciting or interesting, you'll stay awake just to find out how it ends. So perhaps rereading old favorites would be a good idea for a while.

IF IT CAUSES ANXIETY . . .

Some of your hard things may even seem insignificant to others, but *if it causes you anxiety,* then it's part of the hard stuff.

Paying bills and balancing the checkbook may be a hated and bewildering task for you if your spouse always took charge of the money. Fortunately, most banks are happy to teach patrons how to balance their checkbooks. Don't be afraid to ask them for help.

I had paid our bills, so that wasn't a problem for me. But I had trouble remembering to put gas in the car—and I still forget it once in a while. Wayne had always taken care of that. AAA Roadside Assistance continues to help me with the results of my memory lapses.

Keeping the car clean had also been Wayne's responsibility. One week at church, a friend looked critically at my once-white Oldsmobile Omega and said, "Sandy, why don't you wash that thing?"

So, the day before I went to church the next week, I washed the car. Then after church I couldn't find it. I was looking for a light earth-colored car—not a white one. I still frequently forget to wash the car.

Big or small, important or seemingly trivial, we all have hard stuff to do. None of it will go away if we don't do it. No amount of self-pity will complete the tasks or accomplish the deed. So we say a prayer to stiffen our spines and get busy.

There is, however, one hard thing I did that provided a lot of support for my family and relief from some of the cares on my shoulders. I learned to accept help.

LEARNING TO ACCEPT HELP

The suit-and-tie faculty looked at Gary with raised eyebrows. It may have been the end of the freethinking seventies, but this was a conservative Christian college community. According to rumor, Gary delivered his biology lectures sitting cross-legged on his desk, wearing jeans and a caftan—and drinking Pepsi.

Yet it was Gary who came to me at church two weeks after Wayne had died. "Make a list of what needs to be done in the yard that Wayne would be doing if he were still here," he said. "My boys and I will be up at your place about nine o'clock in the morning to take care of it."

They came, and my yard looked beautiful when they left. Gardening had been one of my husband's passions. I, on the other hand, am a rotten gardener. So the timely help from Gary and his sons was of major importance to me.

Notice that Gary didn't ask if I wanted them to come. That's important.

If he had asked, I would have said, "Thank you, but you don't need to do that." He just said, "We're coming." And they did. I still have warm feelings of gratitude when I think of it.

Eight months after Wayne died, the kids and I moved to a house nearer the school they attended and where I taught. Shortly after the move, we decided to hang shelves on either side of the fireplace for our many books. So we bought the brackets and the boards and got out Wayne's circular saw. Then I looked at my son, Ed, and he looked at me. And we stood there. We discovered that neither of us had ever used it— and we were both afraid to try!

Notice THAT GARY DIDN'T ASK IF I WANTED THEM TO COME. THAT'S IMPORTANT. . . . HE JUST SAID, "WE'RE COMING."

Finally, I called Bill, one of my husband's closest friends. When he walked in, he had a big grin on his face. He quickly cut the boards to the length we had marked and helped us put them on the wall brackets. Before he left, he said, "Thank you so much for calling me. I'm glad you did."

He thanked me? For what? For allowing him to spend half an hour in my living room sawing boards—probably delaying his supper?

It took me a while to realize that in his own grief for my husband, he needed to be able to help us. I am so grateful he did.

Learning to accept needed help was difficult for me. I was raised with the motto "It's more blessed to give than to receive." As an adult, I'd been on the giving and sharing end of things. But from the time Wayne first became ill, I had no energy or emotional resources to share with anyone but him. I couldn't seem to get on top of things. Even my two children learned to cope largely on their own, I'm ashamed to say. Actually, the children took over quite a few of the household chores. Young as she was, Kimberly often prepared lunches and took care of loading and unloading the dishwasher. Ed mowed the lawn and sometimes vacuumed the house.

At first when someone offered help to us, I declined—even though we desperately needed help. How could I accept help that I knew I could never repay? It was a hard struggle to just say "Thank you" when someone offered to pick up my dry cleaning, to take a child to the dentist, or to mow the lawn.

It was Bill, that friend of my husband's, who taught me to do it. Once when I was balking at an offer of help, he looked me straight in the eye and said words I'll never forget. "You would deny your friends that good feeling that comes from helping you?"

I remember standing there, staring at him. I'd never thought about it from that perspective. It was like receiving a revelation.

I tried to absorb this new concept, but it wasn't easy. If I accepted the help my friends and acquaintances offered, that meant I wasn't capable of managing my own household, didn't it? Well, I *wasn't* capable right then. I needed their help—needed to learn to accept the help they offered so freely.

Some of our wise friends quit offering help, bless them. They simply informed me of their plans for us. They knew us and our lifestyle well enough to know what would be acceptable and helpful.

When Bill read this manuscript years later, he added further wisdom to it. "You've forgotten something important," he said. "People *want* to help, but most of us don't know what to do. So when you ask for help, it gives people some direction. And it not only gives them pleasure at being able to help, but it gives them the feeling of being needed." He went on to add that people appreciate being asked to help. It tells them that you consider them close, trusted friends.

MISTAKES—THEIRS AND MINE

"You'd better get busy and lose some weight so you can get out there and find yourself another husband," said a woman I barely knew.

I looked at her in shock. My husband had been dead for *only two days*— and I wore a size ten.

I received some other strange comments. You probably will too.

"It must have been his time to go."

"Oh, my goodness! I don't know what I would do if my husband died! It's too much work to get out there and find another one at my age."

"The Lord giveth; the Lord taketh away."

"It's the will of God."

I had the hardest time graciously accepting these last two comments. *Does this mean God arranged for my husband to have cancer? Are they really blaming God for murder—something that people would be put in jail for doing? Are the doctors fighting against God when they try to heal a person?*

Well-meaning people say things they hope will be helpful or comforting. Often they don't really *know* what to say, but they feel they must say something. They haven't learned yet that there's really nothing they can say that will help. The words they choose may hurt, puzzle, and sometimes even repulse, but it is helpful to try to look behind what they say and listen to their hearts.

It IS HELPFUL TO TRY TO LOOK BEHIND WHAT THEY SAY AND LISTEN TO THEIR HEARTS.

Personally, I prefer people saying the wrong things and still being in my life to those who had been friends and who now just stay away.

Before Wayne became sick, we spent many weekend afternoons with Bob and June and their kids (not their real names). We had picnics and went bird-watching together. We took camping trips to the mountains and to the deserts. We were friends. But once Wayne was diagnosed with cancer, they never came near us again. I missed having their strong faith to lean on. I missed the shared lunches, the hikes, and the table games we played with our kids. But even at church, they always seemed to sit as far away from our family as they could get. In a church of twenty-five hundred members, that was quite a distance.

Six years later, I visited the area and attended my previous church. This time I accidentally came face-to-face with June. She smiled rather shyly and said, "I'm so sorry we lost contact with you. When Wayne got cancer, we didn't know what to say or do. So we just stayed away." She smiled again, turned, and slipped away into the crowd. And it was the last time she's spoken to me, even though I've revisited that church occasionally in the years since.

I can't be angry with these friends. Before I experienced death in my own family, I also felt awkward around grieving people. I thought I had to have something wise and comforting to say. Now, I know that I can just ring the doorbell and hold out my arms. Or bring them a new rosebush. Or offer to go grocery shopping for them. Or send a card with an "I care" message on it. I don't need to answer their whys. I couldn't, even if I wanted to.

In spite of the blunders some of my friends made, I loved them. I needed my friends, especially during the rough patches in my life.

The mistakes *I* made were legion. Even now, I keep learning about what I should have done differently. My reactions were, I think, rather typical for many people suffering a tragic loss. Unfortunately, I didn't recognize the pattern until quite a while after my son died—and that was nine years after my husband's death. I must be a slow learner.

One of the mistakes both my husband and I made was staying strong, no matter what, not giving in to natural emotions. I don't believe in wallowing in sadness, but some of us carry the "stiff upper lip" a step too far.

One night I felt the bed shaking. *At last,* I thought, *he's letting go.* I rolled over and silently put my arms around his heaving body. I held him close, trying to think of something appropriate to say.

After a few moments, his voice came out of the darkness. "I don't think you understand," he said. Then he proceeded to tell me of a happening during the day that had struck him as funny! He was laughing—not crying. And I was all geared up to comfort him! I could have hit him.

Shortly after my husband was diagnosed with cancer, I turned into the iron woman. I had to, didn't I? I had children to care for, a life to make for them. Looking back, I think I tried too hard to be strong. A few months after his death, I returned to my iron-woman mentality. Perhaps it would have helped the children if I'd been more vulnerable, and if we'd shared more tears, and if we'd spent more time together at their daddy's grave.

I wish I'd told my husband more of what his death would mean to me. I wish I'd cried in his arms and let him comfort me. It's that iron woman thing again. Actually, we both tried to be strong for each other—too strong. We should have been more vulnerable, in order to allow the other to give comfort.

In SPITE OF THE BLUNDERS SOME OF MY FRIENDS MADE, I LOVED THEM.

One of Wayne's brothers visited for a few days and read a lot to him from the Bible. Wayne really enjoyed that. My brother-in-law suggested I read Wayne a passage from the Bible each day. A great idea—but I found I couldn't do it. If I even thought about it, I'd start crying (and head for the bathroom). I wished I had done it anyway.

After Wayne died, I spent money as if we were rich, trying to fill the empty place in our lives. I bought a new bedroom set for each child—fortunately I had only two. Then we bought a smaller, equally expensive house, closer to the school. We ate out a lot. We traveled. We bought *things*! We acted like there was no tomorrow. And, frankly, for a while I didn't care whether there was or not. So, we went into debt. It took me several years to recover from that spree.

I gained weight. There's no nice way to say it. I replaced many entire meals with a Mars candy bar—sending my stomach into starvation mode and turning me into a chocoholic. Other times I'd nibble—on anything. Sometimes I'd realize I was halfway through eating something I really disliked, such as olives or cooked tomatoes. I gained twenty pounds, and I still didn't miss Wayne any less.

When my twenty-two-year-old son died as a result of a car/truck accident, the cycle began again. My daughter and I went to England for three weeks and then came home and bought a cabin in the woods. So we were in debt again.

And, yes, I nibbled on another twenty pounds. Some folks just don't learn.

FACING LONELINESS

I also dealt with grief at first by changing the subject or activity instead of facing up to it. Even now, over twenty years after the death of my husband, I still do it. When I feel myself getting lonely, I read a book, play computer solitaire, watch baseball on TV, go shopping, eat chocolate, write a book . . .

I'm told by the experts that this is not a healthful way to deal with loneliness. They say I haven't faced my loss. I need to *admit* I'm lonely, to face it head on. Only then is it safe to pursue the activities that help me forget. By admitting the reason behind my behavior, I won't use these activities as a way to run away from reality, they say. I'm sure I would have learned this if I'd attended one of the many grief-recovery classes offered by most hospitals—like my daughter urged me to. Perhaps that is another of my mistakes.

In spite of what the experts say, however, I couldn't pretend Wayne was still alive, as much as I'd have liked to. One thing we're never warned about ahead of time is telephone calls. Business people and old friends from out of town would call and asked, "May I speak to Wayne?" So I had to keep saying it—over and over, "I'm sorry. You can't speak to him because he died two weeks ago."

Actually, the most devastating for me was our high-school reunion. The first person I saw when I entered, asked, "Where's Wayne?" and I burst into tears. Once was enough. I didn't go back for a long, long time.

We each deal with grief in our own ways. But if you can learn from my mistakes, you might be better off. And perhaps less in debt . . . and thinner.

ANOTHER MISTAKE— IGNORING YOUR OWN HEALTH

It's important to pay at least *some* attention to your own personal needs in order to survive as a well-balanced, healthy person. So assess what you personally need to get your life back on a healthy, sane track, and be creative about making it happen.

Just before we found out Wayne's cancer had returned, I had a checkup, and a small lump was discovered on one breast. The doctor told me to watch it,

> *It's* IMPORTANT TO PAY AT LEAST *SOME* ATTENTION TO YOUR OWN PERSONAL NEEDS IN ORDER TO SURVIVE AS A WELL-BALANCED, HEALTHY PERSON.

and if it seemed to be growing, to come back to his office. Well, then we got the news about Wayne's cancer, and I didn't give that little lump another thought. My husband was dying; how could I think about anything else?

Six months after Wayne's death, I glanced in the mirror before going to work. I noticed that my blouse didn't lay right across my chest. Lightly touching my chest, I was stunned. If half a golf ball had been taped there, it wouldn't have felt any bigger. I phoned the doctor, and after a brief examination, I ended up in the hospital having a mastectomy. If I'd just paid attention to my own health as the doctor had advised me, I'd have caught the tumor soon enough to avoid that kind of surgery and the fourteen months of chemotherapy that followed—and avoided the additional trauma for my children.

Other survivors tell me they should have rested more—especially during the first few weeks after the death of a loved one. They tried to accomplish everything that needed doing—instead of relying on family and friends to make some of the decisions. Then they finally went to bed in

So TAKE GOOD CARE OF YOURSELF, EVEN IN THE MIDST OF YOUR PAIN. EAT RIGHT—EVEN IF THE FOOD TASTES LIKE SAWDUST. AND BE SURE TO GET ENOUGH REST.

complete exhaustion. After a few weeks of this, their health began to suffer.

So take good care of yourself, even in the midst of your pain. Eat right—even if the food tastes like sawdust. And be sure to get enough rest.

SHARING RESPONSIBILITIES

We all find ourselves with our own set of responsibilities, stresses, and priorities. Are they all necessary and unavoidable? Will the world fall apart if you don't carry out a certain duty?

Take a good look at all your responsibilities. Is it possible to simplify your life? If you have children and they are old enough, can they accept some responsibility?

Take a good look at all your responsibilities. Is it possible to simplify your life?

For example, a small child might be responsible for taking out the trash and feeding the pets. An older child might vacuum the house. A teen might keep the car washed and the tank full. And there's yard work and housework chores to share.

I learned a lot about job-sharing from that old, semibiographical movie

Belles on Their Toes. Remember it? The mother, Lillian Gilbreth, is a new widow with *twelve* children. In a family meeting, the children discuss the household duties with Mrs. Gilbreth. Each child decides what he or she can do to keep their home operating smoothly, so their mother can resume her career and support them. One of the oldest children takes over the management of the family finances: paying bills, depositing money, and ordering supplies. Several older ones take over the care of the youngest ones. Another two or three agree to clean the house.

I have nothing but admiration for a woman who can keep track

> For my family, it took more than six months before we really got down to planning and dividing up the work.

of twelve children, run a home, and handle a career. And she was even written about in encyclopedias!

For my family, it took more than six months before we really got down to planning and dividing up the work. My kids learned to wash their own clothes and each took charge of one evening meal every week. They kept the wastebaskets emptied, and they helped me clean house and do the yard work. It worked for us for as long as I was consistent in my expectations— at least for a while.

ADJUSTING PRIORITIES

Are your priorities straight? We have to look for causes of unnecessary stress in our lives and adjust our priorities.

As a new widow, I returned to work for the first time in fourteen years, and within that first year, I began taking chemotherapy treatments for my own cancer recovery. As a result, I didn't handle things very well at home. My communication with my children soon consisted of orders. Mow the lawn. Do the dishes. Dust the furniture. For heaven's sake, take out the trash.

For the first time since they were born, I screamed at my kids—for no reason that I can remember. I even took a swing at them once or twice. Apologizing to your children is difficult, but necessary sometimes.

My sister visited us and assessed the situation tersely. "Why don't you get yourself a housekeeper?"

We found a junior-high girl who would come in two hours a week and do the basic cleaning. What a blessing that was! My life began to get back on an even keel. Just the removal of that one pressure made a big difference for us. Call it a realignment of my priorities.

What about *your* priorities? Decide what's important for you and your family and keep that in mind as you attempt to simplify your complicated life. If a responsibility or an experience is causing you greater stress than you feel you can handle, take a long look at it. Is it important to you? If it's not high on your list of priorities, perhaps it shouldn't be part of your life at this time.

Decide WHAT'S IMPORTANT FOR YOU AND YOUR FAMILY AND KEEP THAT IN MIND AS YOU ATTEMPT TO SIMPLIFY YOUR COMPLICATED LIFE. IF A RESPONSIBILITY OR AN EXPERIENCE IS CAUSING YOU GREATER STRESS THAN YOU FEEL YOU CAN HANDLE, TAKE A LONG LOOK AT IT.

For five years or so, I had been in charge of a room full of eight-year-olds at my church. Right after my husband's death, I walked in to this room and burst into tears. I had full responsibility for my children at home, and I had full responsibility for my class of fifth-graders at school. My church job was one added responsibility that I just couldn't handle anymore. But doing church work is a good thing, right? I felt so guilty when I resigned that position. It's hard to back out of something you've been responsible for and that you enjoy. I know. But sometimes even doing good works can be too much for you—especially in the early days of your grief.

One of the most valuable sentences I learned in those days was, "Thank you for asking me, but no, not this time."

MORE ABOUT PRIORITIES

Soon after I became a widow, my eight-year-old daughter said, "Mama, if you get married again, I'm gonna run away from home."

No, I don't think she was being selfish—just observant. Several of her friends had stepfathers who appeared to be unpleasant fellows. Later, when she was a teenager, her priorities changed. "Mom, why don't you marry a rich man so we can have a swimming pool?"

I decided early on that remarriage was not a priority issue for me. In fact, I remember telling the Lord, "If You want me to get married again, that's *Your* responsibility. I've got lots of other things I need Your help with."

Though I have a few male friends, the Lord has never tapped me on the shoulder, pointed to one, and said, "Here, marry this one." So I've gone on my merry way, concentrating on the things that have become important to me.

To those of you for whom remarriage *is* a priority, I have only one caution: *Take your time.* During the first year or so after your spouse's death, you get so lonely that it's easy to mistake your feelings. Some of my friends have regretted their hasty marriages.

I remember the first man who took me out to dinner after my husband's death—eighteen months after. For the first time since about six months *before* I became a widow, someone was taking care of *me*. Someone was paying attention to me as a *woman*—not just as a mother or a caregiver or a widow. It was a heady feeling. I was sure I was in love again. A phone call to my long-suffering sister helped me straighten my thinking. I am *sooooo* grateful that no one asked me to marry him during those first years. I'm sure I would have said "Yes" because I was lonely—not a good foundation for a marriage. And I have become content now with my single life.

> *I've* GONE ON MY MERRY WAY, CONCENTRATING ON THE THINGS THAT HAVE BECOME IMPORTANT TO ME.

I chose to make my children my top priority—not my whole life, mind you, but my top priority. I wanted to make life meaningful for them. I wanted to give them a full life, even though it would be without their beloved daddy.

If you have children, you're fortunate. Planning for them will move your focus off yourself. They will still bring joy to your life and occupation to your hands.

Watch that your children don't get shoved aside while adult mourners take center stage. They need an extra measure of security during this time of grieving and rebuilding. They need to know they are important to you, by actions as well as words. So spend quality time with them, take them places, do things together, and concentrate on them.

I was eating breakfast with my daughter and granddaughter at a cozy Village Inn once and saw something I've never forgotten.

A mother came in with two children, perhaps eight and ten years old. As soon as they ordered, she got on the cell phone—and stayed on it for the entire meal. Her children sat across from her, looking forlorn. By her actions, she conveyed to the children how unimportant they were in her life. I could have wept for them.

BACK TO WORK

Most of us are not independently wealthy; work is essential. If you have been working, this won't change for you. For those of you who were stay-at-home wives, things will be different. If you've had some career training, you have an advantage. Chances are you will be working at a job you can enjoy.

I taught elementary school before I chose to stay home and be a full-time wife and mother. After fourteen years out of the classroom, I returned to teaching with some fear and trepidation—but with a lot of prayer and encouragement from friends, I managed to pull it off.

Two years after Wayne's death, I considered making a change in my career. I discussed this prospect with my children. Together we decided that I should work on a master's degree one evening a week, so that ultimately we would have more money coming into our bank account, and I might have a different job in the education field. They were ten and fifteen years old by then, and we had a big dog, so I felt secure letting them stay home alone.

My career, in a sense, belonged to all of us. Ideally, a group decision brings group cooperation. And my children were old enough to have some valuable input in this decision-making experience.

A word of warning, however: Don't get so caught up in your career and in making money that your kids end up grieving for the loss of *both* parents. They do need *you*.

Married Friends—Some Hard Truths

Throughout this book, you can't help but notice how important friends were to my survival. I would be sticking my head in the sand, however, if I didn't mention one very real stress you may encounter. I didn't have this particular problem—either because I am lucky in my friends—or because I'm not one of the world's "beautiful people," so my friends never thought about it. But many newly widowed (or divorced women) have told me they have had to

Some FOLKS ARE SO INSECURE IN THEIR MARRIAGE RELATIONSHIPS THAT WHEN A FRIEND BECOMES SINGLE, SHE OR HE IS NOW LOOKED AT AS "THE COMPETITION."

face it—and the other day a widower told me that he faced the same issue.

To put it bluntly, some folks are so insecure in their marriage relationships that when a friend becomes single, she or he is now looked at as "the competition." Many people who have lost their spouses find themselves unwelcome in the homes of some of their formerly close friends.

I just mention this so you will be prepared if it happens to you. There isn't a lot you can do about it, except perhaps confine your social interactions with that friend to shopping and lunches until she decides you aren't a husband stealer.

On the other hand, we need to be sure that, in our loneliness

If YOU THINK ONLY OF YOURSELF AND THE BAD THINGS THAT HAVE HAPPENED TO YOU, YOU WON'T *LIVE*— ONLY EXIST. . . . LOOK AT YOUR RESPONSIBILITIES, YOUR INTERESTS, AND YOUR VALUES. AND EVEN LOOK AT WHAT MAKES YOU SMILE.

for male company, we don't flirt with, or rely too heavily on, someone else's husband, giving his wife a good reason for pulling away from us.

As I discussed my own priorities in the previous few sections, I hope you were inspired to look closely at *your* life. If you think only of yourself and the bad things that have happened to you, you won't *live*—only exist. You'll just wallow in self-pity and never move on. Look at your responsibilities, your interests, and your values. And even look at what makes you smile. Then decide how you are going to live the rest of your life— with the emphasis on *living*.

FILLING THE EMPTY HOLE

"Do you know what I will always remember when I think about Wayne?" Pastor Darold asked during his visit the night Wayne died. "I'll remember our camping trips with college students and faculty families. We'd be out hiking, and I'd look up and see Wayne squatting down to show some small child a flower or an animal hole or an insect."

Several other visitors related their own memories of Wayne. I sat there amazed. My

In SHARING THEIR SPECIAL MEMORIES, THEY WERE GIVING ME BACK A LITTLE PIECE OF THE MAN I'D JUST LOST.

husband had just died six or seven hours earlier, and when these people showed up one by one at my door, I felt dismay. I thought I needed to be alone with my family.

It took me a while to realize the wonderful thing that was happening. In sharing their special memories, they were giving me back a little piece of the man I'd just lost. They began filling that empty hole in my life—a hole that I was scarcely aware of yet.

Our church-going habit accented another hole: the empty place in the third pew from the front on the right-hand side. Three of us sat together now—not four. It didn't seem right. Sitting beside friends or grandparent-type people, or even sitting in a different section of the church helped a little—but not much.

As LIFE GOES ON AND YEARS PASS, THAT HOLE STILL EMERGES WHEN I LEAST EXPECT IT.

As life goes on and years pass, that hole still emerges when I least expect it.

"I wish Dad were here," Ed told me the summer after his freshman year in college. "I'd really like to talk to him. I need his advice."

My son was struggling to decide on a career path. He wanted a man—his dad—to talk to. Sometimes a grandfather or favorite uncle can step into this gap. In my son's case, I suggested he talk to his major professor, a man he held in high esteem, and one with whom he had developed a friendship.

Often friends are willing to help; they just may be waiting for you to make the first move. Ask God to guide you to the right people.

TRY SOMETHING NEW

Our home seemed so empty after Wayne died. Granted, there was still a mom, two kids, a cat, and a dog, but our home—our lives—felt pretty empty.

One evening we ate supper with a grandmotherly lady who owned a white cockatiel. "Be careful of Tweety," she warned. "He used to be so friendly; now I can't get near him without getting bitten."

As the evening progressed, Ed lost interest in the "woman talk" and sat down on the floor near the birdcage. An hour later when I glanced over at him, Ed sat with his

Our INTEREST IN THE "OUTSIDE" WORLD REKINDLES, AND WE BECOME INTERESTING PEOPLE AGAIN.

hand in the cage—with Tweety perched on his hand. The lady was amazed. When we left, she asked Ed to take the bird home and continue to work with him until Tweety was really tame again.

So that's how it started. Within six months, Ed was taming Amazon parrots for a bird farm. And then I bought him a young parrot of his own. He tamed it, sold it, and bought two. And he repeated the process. Soon we had three large parrot stands in our small living room, through which rotated a variety of Amazon parrots, a few cockatoos, and an African gray parrot.

Volunteering WILL BRING FRIENDS, OCCUPATION, AND A SENSE OF BEING NEEDED— AND WILL TAKE YOUR FOCUS OFF YOURSELF.

Before the year was up, we also had a walk-in aviary in the backyard for Ed's finches and cockatiels to breed in. And that didn't include Kimberly's pet cockatiel or my finches.

We did go overboard, I'll admit. But it kept us busy—very busy. It was fun for the kids, and our house didn't seem quite so empty. It at least partially filled that empty hole made by Wayne's absence.

If you don't have children or if you live alone, perhaps you need to focus your life in a different direction. And if you're retired and without the social interaction of a job, life can be lonely.

Also, living alone brings problems when we're grieving. It's easy to pull into ourselves and think only of our own sadness and loss. If our conversations stay on a one-note song about what "used to be" or "if only," even our best friends and grown children will soon visit reluctantly, only out of duty.

By taking classes, doing volunteer work, or even cooking lunch for a few other lonely friends, we begin to be alive. Our interest in the "outside" world rekindles, and we become interesting people again.

Search FOR SOMETHING THAT INTERESTS YOU, SOMETHING YOU CAN BE ENTHUSIASTIC ABOUT. THEN GO FOR IT. YOU'LL BE HAPPIER, HEALTHIER, AND CERTAINLY MORE INTERESTED IN LIFE.

Consider offering your services to organizations such as the American Cancer Society, Goodwill, or a hospice. Volunteers are also needed in hospitals, schools, and community service organizations. The possibilities are endless. In fact, my local paper, the *Oregonian,* carries a column every Thursday headlined "Volunteers." Check your own paper for an item like this. Volunteering will bring friends, occupation, and a sense of being needed—and will take your focus off yourself. Who can sink into depression knowing you are needed so desperately, and knowing that you can bring joy and help to someone who would otherwise not have it? Activities like this will keep you from looking inward too much and feeling sorry for yourself.

How about taking a class at your community college? The offerings are diverse enough to appeal to almost everyone's taste and interest. Our local community college offers line dancing, watercolor painting, bookkeeping, and self-defense in addition to classes on antiques, herbs, memoir writing, and archery.

If you're comfortable with the computer, what about finding an appropriate chatroom? Lots of people find encouragement and understanding by communicating with strangers who are handling the same problems they are.

The computer opens up other channels too. I have a friend who used his computer to trace his family tree back to the 1600s. He has met (by e-mail or in person) several long-lost relatives. It's been an exciting adventure for him.

Search for something that interests you, something you can be enthusiastic about. Then go for it. You'll be happier, healthier, and certainly more interested in life—and more interesting to be with.

BUILDING NEW MEMORIES AND EXPLORING NEW SCENES

We started with little things. We had always eaten home-cooked meals, so now we went to Taco Bell or Denny's occasionally. We had played Sorry and Stratego, so now we played Monopoly.

A year after Wayne died, we really broke loose. We found one of those train-travel bargains in which I paid full fare, my son was half fare, and my daughter was a quarter fare. So we planned—and took—a train trip across the United States. We had friends near Philadelphia, so we got off the train there. For a few weeks, they showed us around Pennsylvania, with a

> A YEAR AFTER WAYNE DIED, . . . WE PLANNED—AND TOOK—A TRAIN TRIP ACROSS THE UNITED STATES.

side trip to Washington, D.C. Not exactly in the Philadelphia area—but a lot closer than it was from our home in California. Then we rented a small car, and the three of us headed northeast. We picked out a small town on the coast of Maine—chosen because of its unpronounceable name—and drove to it.

Ogunquit, Maine, was a delightful little lobstering village. We stayed at Captain Perkins' Bed and Breakfast, a quaint inn with a history. We spent three days there, visiting antique shops, searching for old straight-edged razors for my son's collection and for additions to my daughter's cat collection.

Search YOUR IMAGINATION FOR NEW ACTIVITIES THAT YOU'D LIKE TO TRY.

In Massachusetts we stayed with former California neighbors who took us for a memorable day in Boston. We got acquainted with the Old North Church, Quincy Market, and funnel cakes.

We were gone about a month altogether and came home with lots of fun new memories, ready to begin the next school year.

Later, my five-year teaching appointment in Singapore offered more new travel opportunities. The pay wasn't great, but the travel benefits were outstanding. So my children and I were able to go through Europe on our way home two different times. We took full advantage of it.

You may not like fast-food restaurants, traveling, or parrots, but search your imagination for new activities that you'd like to try, which will add excitement and interest to your day-to-day experiences. Where have you always wanted to go? What have you always wanted to try? Here are a few ideas to get you started, many of which we tried.

- Raise parrots
- Paint a mural on the bedroom wall
- Make a video
- Take up rock collecting
- Catch lizards
- Join a wood-carving class
- Learn to play the banjo
- Plant three kinds of tomatoes
- Breed dogs
- Visit your state capitol
- Attend a baseball game
- Redecorate your living room
- Learn ham radio
- Build a family Web site
- Take piano lessons
- Learn to quilt

We spent several really enjoyable evenings by each drawing a floor plan for our "dream house." No architect could have made heads or tails of them, but we enjoyed the activity. My son's plan always included an outdoor aviary for his parrots that was bigger than the living space for people.

None of this means you won't miss your loved one. Definitely not. I even shed tears in Paris, thinking of how my husband would have laughed at our activities, and I missed his reassuring presence. But it does mean that you are getting on with life, forming new and different bonds with your restructured family, or learning what it's like to take care of yourself and be independent again.

VACATIONS

If you are in the habit of taking vacations, this may be a tough hole to fill. Vacations are such family-oriented events. We need to think of things to do and places to go that don't constantly remind us of the missing loved one. That's a tall order.

Our family-of-four vacations were usually camping trips. Since Wayne's death, I've been camping only once, when my daughter's third-grade class went on a camp-out in the autumn

As a single mom, I eventually needed a vacation—a real vacation.

after my husband died. Because her teacher was my friend, she invited my son and me to go along. For my children, it was a time of warm memories, comfortable familiarity, and fun with friends. For me, it was an emotional, anguished-filled three days. Everything reminded me of camping with Wayne. It intensified my loss. I never went camping again.

Instead, the next summer we took the train trip to Pennsylvania that I mentioned in the previous section, and later, another train trip to Mexico City. If we did go to the desert or the mountains, we stayed in cabins. We needed to make new memories in new places.

Vacations hold still another complication for a single parent. A vacation never offers the opportunity to truly relax. We still have to care for the children; keep track of their clothes; either make or arrange for meals; and be responsible for the family activities, transportation, and behavior. Even if your children are old enough to take some responsibility for themselves, it's still not a really relaxing vacation.

As a single mom, I eventually needed a vacation—a real vacation.

I don't know how it began, but a year or so after my husband died, my sister and I came up with the idea of a four-day (three-night) vacation. We managed to escape alone for these much needed respites from responsibility almost every year until the children were grown.

What we did wasn't important. We often ended up sitting on the floor of some out-of-the-way used-book store, discovering new treasures we just couldn't live without or eavesdropping on passersby from a sidewalk deli. Sometimes we took in a musical. One time we took a boat to Catalina Island and returned by helicopter. The worst part of the helicopter trip was when the pilot asked how much we each weighed so he'd know how to balance the load. (My weight is the only thing in my life I lie about!)

We usually didn't plan very far ahead; we just did whatever we felt like doing. Neither of us had much money, so we didn't usually go shopping—except in bookstores. We tried to be creative—as well as casual. Once, we turned a seven-hour trip from Southern California to the San Francisco

We USUALLY DIDN'T PLAN VERY FAR AHEAD; WE JUST DID WHATEVER WE FELT LIKE DOING.

Airport into a four-day relaxing adventure. Each time we took off on one of these jaunts, I returned refreshed, renewed, and ready to take up my normal responsibilities. We still enjoy an occasional minivacation—even though now we are both widowed grandmothers.

Travel agencies and clubs often plan short tours to interesting places. So

if you don't have a sister like mine or a best friend who can get away, a tour offers ready-made companionship and security.

Single parents really *need* to get away from their children once in a while. Married people can trade off when one parent becomes tired or frustrated. As widowed parents, we don't have that option.

No matter how educated or kind or Christian we may be, we still have buttons the kids can—and do—push. Then we

Don't OVERLOOK THE LITTLE THINGS THAT ADD QUALITY TO YOUR EVERYDAY LIFE.

have to consciously do something to keep our cool: take a walk around the block; stand alone on the back porch and count robins; or lock the bathroom door, turn on the shower, and cry. And, occasionally, take a four-day vacation.

If you have young children, but don't have a grandma or aunt in the neighborhood who is willing to stay with the children so you can get away, perhaps you can do a little child-care trading until someone you trust owes you three or four days.

Don't overlook the little things that add quality to your everyday life: lunch with a friend, a book by a favorite author, or a TV program from the History Channel instead of the cartoon channel your kids like to watch. Think of these as minivacations.

Reaching Out

I've included this section last because somewhere down the road to recovery, you may find that reaching out to help others is the best way to further your own healing process. And *you* will receive the wonderful feeling that comes when you've helped ease someone else's pain. Who better to offer a helping hand to a suffering friend than one who's been through the experience?

I was excited recently to find this Bible text: "What a wonderful God we have . . . [he] so wonderfully comforts and strengthens us in our hardships and trials. And why does he do this? So that when others are troubled, needing our sympathy and encouragement, *we can pass on to them this same help and comfort* God has given us" (2 Corinthians 1:3, 4, TLB; emphasis added).

It was not a conscious action on my part. I certainly wasn't thinking about helping others when I was in the midst of my own tragedies. But later, when I thought about it, the memories and ideas came—memories of the helpful and comforting things people had said and done for me.

These helpful deeds don't require a huge outlay of funds or a technical degree. They may not even take much time. Sit back and think a minute. What did someone do for you that you especially appreciated? Or what small thing did you wish someone had done for you? Did you long for someone to take your children on an outing and give you an afternoon to yourself? Did you wish someone would just come to visit? Return your library books? Invite your family over for supper? Wash your car?

Remember ALSO THE *APPROACH* YOU APPRECIATED.

Remember also the *approach* you appreciated. When someone said, "Call me if you need anything," did you? Of course not. If you know the grieving person well enough to know what would be acceptable, decide what you can do and how to go about it; then just do it. This is especially good in the early days of grief, when the mind is still foggy or exhausted by grief. For others, you might say, "I'm coming over to help you.

Would you prefer me to wash windows or go to the supermarket for you?" And by the way, you'll probably cry right along with them the first few times, and that's OK.

The important thing is that you are helping a friend to survive. After all, that is the only possible form of payback for all the nice things people did for you. And it is another step on the road to healing.

Recounting some of the ways people have helped me will, I hope, have given you some ideas of how you might help others in need. Here are a few more.

This recital should really begin two years before Wayne's death, the day the chemistry department

My FRIEND GAVE ME THE COURAGE AND SUPPORT I NEEDED.

had scheduled our annual family day at the beach. Wayne got up early to put another row of shingles on the garage roof before we left. He'd snatched bits of time all week to get it reroofed. He had one side almost finished.

I was leisurely stretching and thinking about getting up when I heard a scream and a crash. Flying to the back door, I saw my husband and the ladder both lying on the patio.

"Shall I call an ambulance?" I asked stupidly.

"No," he said as he crawled into the house, huge beads of sweat rolling down his face.

I ran to the phone and called my nurse-friend, Priscilla. "We're coming," she said. What she actually did was call an ambulance and a doctor and arrange for someone to come get our children—before she and her husband left home.

The rest is still a bit fuzzy in my mind. But hours later, Clyde and Priscilla stood beside me to hear the doctor use some fancy words that basically meant Wayne had a broken back. Then they drove me home, picking up the kids on the way.

I will never forget what I saw as we pulled into the driveway. The entire chemistry department was on the roof—hammering shingles. They never said, "May we?" or "Call if you need help." They just did it.

That was one year before my husband was diagnosed with colon cancer.

Before Wayne became bedridden, friends made it possible for him to do a few things he longed to do. For instance, he had read lots of books about earthquake fault lines. When we camped in the desert, he always searched out the places he'd read about. So his friend Jerry took a day off work to fly Wayne fault-hunting in a small plane. They spent a happy day looking for—and at—fault lines. In Southern California, that's an easy thing to do. For Wayne, it was a very special day.

We even went camping several times, another activity he loved. Friends took us in their motor home; Wayne was too weak for tent camping.

As his cancer advanced, Wayne became jaundiced. His yellow-tinted skin itched constantly. The only relief he got was when lotion was rubbed into his skin. Several friends developed the habit of stopping in to visit with him, rubbing lotion on his arms and legs as they talked. This gave me a respite—and a chance to go to the grocery store.

Wayne's good friend and colleague Lee came one morning and spread chemistry books all over Wayne's bed. The two spent three happy hours choosing the best book for the physical chemistry class Lee would be teaching in Wayne's stead the following September. Not only did this activity give me another chance to do the grocery run, but it gave Wayne so much pleasure to know that even though he could no longer teach, he could still contribute his expertise.

My husband wanted to remain at home as long as possible. So, on doctor's orders, nurse friends set up a plant pole in the bedroom and hung an IV bag from it. They taught me how to change the bags.

The day finally came when Wayne had to be admitted to the hospital. The painkiller I could administer wasn't strong enough any more. And he was failing fast.

The next day, a sweet mother-friend took me to see Wayne for a few hours and then took me to a funeral home to begin making arrangements. This wasn't a nightmare; this was real. Wayne's death was coming soon. I wanted to run away, to scream, to punch the soft-spoken lady at the funeral home right in her tight little mouth.

Instead, my friend gave me the courage and support I needed. Without her, I'd have had no plans for Wayne's funeral when he died two days later. And while we attended to business, strange and wonderful things were happening at my house. My friends had connived together to give me help I desperately needed but would have refused.

You see, during the last few months of Wayne's suffering, for two reasons, I had done very little house cleaning. The sound of the vacuum annoyed him (and his Demerol), and I was emotionally exhausted most of the time.

So, can you imagine my shock when I returned home from our visit to the funeral home to a clean house? In my bedroom I found every vestige of sickroom removed—the plant pole that held IVs, the box of syringes, and the medicine bottles. The furniture was rearranged, and on the bed was a bright, new flowery spread. Matching curtains hung at the windows.

Just THE FACT THAT YOU CARE ENOUGH TO WANT TO HELP IS PRICELESS. . . . WHO BETTER TO HELP THAN ONE WHO HAS BEEN THROUGH IT ALL.

The whole house was spotless. Even my eight-year-old daughter's *closet* was clean! Four wonderful elementary school teachers on vacation did this for me. I was overwhelmed. I threw myself across the new bedspread and cried. Later, I found a note on the kitchen counter that read, "Supper's in the fridge."

The day Wayne died I sat beside him and held his hand while he struggled to breathe. Clyde and Priscilla and two young relatives, Ken and Virginia, stood silently near the bed as he gave up the struggle. It couldn't have been easy for any of them, but their support and love meant a lot to me. Shortly after someone took me home, my sister arrived. I found out a few years later that Priscilla had been in touch with her and had told her that Wayne couldn't last the day. So my sister and her son grabbed the first flight heading south from Sacramento.

That night, another friend showed up and asked my kids what they wanted for breakfast the next day. Much to my chagrin, they couldn't agree. One asked for pancakes, the other, waffles. My friend arrived the next morning with both.

That afternoon, my cousin Marie called from Portland, Oregon. "Shall I come for the funeral, or would you like me to come later?"

I looked helplessly at my sister. I couldn't seem to make decisions just then. "Later," she said.

"Later," I repeated into the phone. So Marie came as the other relatives were leaving, and stayed for a week. She cooked, cleaned, and washed. In other words, she kept our home running while we struggled to cope with our grief.

My niece Marilynn came just as Marie left. She kept our home running for another week or so. I remember little about their visits, except that there was always food on the table and our clothes were clean. And once, Marie rescued me from a strange lady I'd never met who seemed to think I was out to ensnare her ex-husband!

The night after Marilynn left, my English neighbor Helen phoned to say she was coming over. Just after the kids went to bed, when I would be really alone for the first time since Wayne's death, Helen arrived bearing a gallon jar of tea.

For two or three hours, we drank tea, and she listened to me recount the whole story of Wayne's illness and death—over and over. For me, it was therapeutic; for her, it must have been extremely boring. But she didn't stop me. She didn't make suggestions. She didn't offer solutions. She didn't tell me things would get better. We drank tea; I talked; she listened.

The fact that I don't even *like* tea never entered my mind.

Few of these ideas require special training; most need only a willing spirit. Just the fact that you care enough to want to help is priceless. And who better to help than one who has been through it all. So, when you feel like you are ready, invite a new widow to lunch, or bring her bubble bath and a good book and take her children to the park. She will feel your caring spirit. And . . . you are healing.

APPENDIX

BOOKS THAT HELPED ME

The Will of God
by Leslie Weatherhead (Nashville, Tenn.: Abingdon Press, 1972).

I never read sermons. But these are different. They were written and delivered by a Church of England minister in the 1940s when Hitler's bombs were dropping on London. This book reminds me that I can still find God, even when everything is in ruins around me.

Good Grief
by Granger E. Westberg (Minneapolis, Minn.: Fortress Press, 1971).

This book describes what happens to people when they grieve. It also helps people to understand how grief experiences and health are related. It is a guide for turning destructive grief into good grief.

The Books I Wish I Had Read

Aarvy Aardvark Finds Hope
by Donna R. O'Toole (Burnsville, N. C.: Mountain Rainbow Publications, 1988).

"A read aloud story for people of all ages about loving and losing, friendship and hope." This blurb from the title page says it all.

Keys to Helping Children Deal With Death and Grief
by Joy Johnson (Hauppauge, N. Y.: Barron's Educational Series, Inc. 1999).

I wished I'd had this book to help me. It even tells you what kind of grief responses to expect from different aged children.

Living When a Loved One Has Died
by Earl A. Grollman (Ypsilanti, Mich.: Beacon Press, 1977).

Grief Recovery
by Larry Yeagley (self-published by the author, 1981).

The Healing Power of Love

Jerry D. Thomas

To Jesus, no human is worthless. When He met those who had fallen completely under Satan's control with no hope of escape, He offered help with gentle kindness. Jesus healed people's minds, spirits, and bodies. The healing power of love went out from Him from the time He was a child.   0-8163-2382-8   Saddle-stitched

Messiah

Jerry D. Thomas

This contemporary adaptation of Ellen White's *The Desire of Ages* brings the classic work on the life of Christ to today's readers of all ages.   0-8163-2334-8   Saddle-stitched